BRITAIN SINCE 1930

Life at Home

Philip Sauvain

WAYLAND

BRITAIN SINCE 1930

The Advance of Technology
Leisure Time
Life at Home
Life at Work

Cover pictures: (Above) A family around the fireside in the 1930s (note the open fire), (below left) a family in the 1980s (note the gas fire), (below right) a schoolboy having breakfast in the 1990s.

Title page: The Prince of Wales paid a surprise visit to poor houses in the East End of London to see for himself the living conditions in slumland. The photo shows Mrs Livesey with her baby, reading the news of the Prince's visit in 1932.

Contents page: An advert for houses in Kent, 1933.

Series editor: Francesca Motisi
Series designer: Joyce Chester
Production Controller: Carol Titchener

© Copyright 1995 Wayland (Publishers) Limited

British Library Cataloguing in Publication Data
Sauvain, Philip
  Life at Home. - (Britain since 1930 series)
  I. Title II. Series
  941.082

ISBN 0-7502-1639-5

Printed and bound by B.P.C. Paulton Books, Great Britain

Picture acknowledgements
The publishers would like to thank the following for allowing their photographs to be reproduced in this book: The Hulton-Deutsch Collection 5 (below), 9, 14 (below), 22 (both), 24 (both), 26 (both), 27; Nottinghamshire County Library 5 (above); Rex Features 23 (bottom right/Bernard Beirne); The Robert Opie Collection *contents page*, 3, 8 (above), 12 (above), 15 (left); Philip Sauvain 6, 7 (below), 8, 10 (both), 11, 15 (right), 16, 19, 20, 21 (both), 23 (top right), 28, 29; Stobhill NHS Trust (Glasgow Hospital) 12 (below); Topham Picturepoint *title page*, 4, 13, 14 (above), 17, 18 (both), 23 (top left), 25.

Contents

SUPER 1933 HOMES

BARNEHURST PARK ESTATE
BARNEHURST, KENT

Estate Office : Station Approach, Barnehurst, Kent.
Telephone : Bexleyheath 406.

9'6 WEEKLY
£395 FREEHOLD

NEW IDEAL HOMESTEADS LTD
BRITAIN'S BIGGEST BUILDERS

Better living conditions

What life was like at home in the 1930s depended on whether you were poor or not. One in four families lived in poverty then. For those without a job – over two million of them in the 1930s – life at home was a struggle to keep warm, get enough food and clothe the children. The areas hardest hit were the coalfields of the north and west of England. Photographs and eyewitness accounts tell us about their homes. They show what it was like to be poor at that time.

Mother and children in a slum dwelling in London in 1932. ⇩

A terraced house in a Yorkshire mill town in 1939

'They were grimy little back-to-back houses, built of red brick, and blackened by soot. They clung to the steeply sloping sides of a cobbled street which led to a woollen mill in the valley bottom. My friend Carter lived halfway up. There were six in his family and their house was 'a two-up and two-down'. A coalfire was always burning in the grate, winter and summer. It was their only source of heat and only means of cooking and boiling water.'

The back yard

'Carter's family had an earth toilet outside in the stone-flagged yard which they shared with their neighbours. Old newspapers hung up inside instead of toilet paper and an icy wind blew under the door in winter. They got their water from an outside tap next to a very smelly dustbin. Lines of soot-begrimed washing hung down across the yard and even across the street. The soot came from their own fire and from the town's mill chimneys.'

⇧ A courtyard in the slums of Nottingham in 1931.

⇦ Despite poor living conditions, many people did their utmost to keep their homes as clean as possible – even to the extent of scrubbing the pavement outside!

5

The appalling conditions of the slums first really came to the notice of many people at the start of the Second World War. When hundreds of thousands of city children were evacuated in September 1939, middle-class families in the countryside who gave them a home were often badly shocked.

Women's Institute report about evacuees in 1940

'Except for a small number the children were filthy. They were unbathed for months. One child was suffering from scabies and the others had dirty septic sores all over their bodies. Their clothing was in a deplorable condition, some of the children being literally sewn into their ragged little garments.'

Living conditions improved after the end of the Second World War – due in part to the work of German bombers. The worst slums were close to the docks and factories where people worked. Many of these were destroyed when Britain's industrial towns were bombed in 1940–42. When the Second World War ended in 1945, millions of new homes were needed.

Air-raid damage left large patches of waste ground in the cities. It took years before these areas could be redeveloped and the poorer houses replaced by new homes. This photograph was taken in Lambeth, London, ten years after the end of the war. ⇩

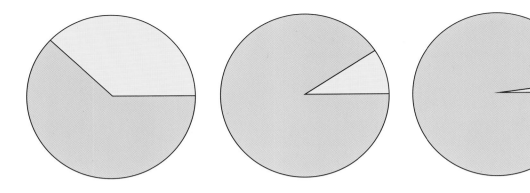

⇦ These graphs compare the number of homes in the United Kingdom without baths in (left) 1951, (middle) 1971, and (right) 1993.

Other things, too, helped to improve the conditions in which people lived. Families were getting smaller so people needed fewer rooms. Children were much more likely to have a bed or even a bedroom to themselves. Many more women went out to work, so family incomes were higher. Even so, government reports after the Second World War showed that large numbers of homes were still without the basic necessities of life, such as an indoor flushing toilet.

After 1950, vast sums of money were spent on clearing the slums and erecting new homes in their place. Many of these were tower blocks of flats with modern conveniences, such as a bathroom, central heating, gas and electricity.

Slum clearance in Sheffield in 1964.
⇩

New homes

Three million new homes were built in the 1930s by private builders. Many of these were built in the London area, the Midlands and the south-east, where people were prospering. Cheaper cars and the growth of bus and electric tram services made it possible for many people to live at a distance from their work. This is why many new homes were built on the main roads leading out of town. As a result, long lines of detached and semi-detached houses stretched out into the country. This was called ribbon development.

A detached house in 1939

'It had a deep bay window on one side at the front and a long, narrow garden at the back. There was stained glass in a window above the front door. The walls were covered in pebble dash. The feature which fascinated us as children – and annoyed my mother – was the bellpush in the wall in the lounge and another at the side of the bath. They had been installed by the previous owner, an elderly lady, to call the servant from the kitchen.'

SUPER **1933** HOMES

BARNEHURST PARK ESTATE
BARNEHURST, KENT
Estate Office : Station Approach, Barnehurst, Kent.
Telephone : Bexleyheath 406.
9'6 WEEKI
£39 FREEHO
NEW IDEAL HOMESTEADS LT
BRITAIN'S BIGGEST BUILDERS

⇧ An advert for new houses in Kent, 1933.

Ribbon development along a main road leading out of a country town. ⇩

8

Some slums were cleared before the Second World War and tall ten-storey blocks of flats built in their place.

New flats in London in 1935

'A modern working-class flat is usually in a block so sited as to obtain the maximum of sunshine. Progress has been made in designing the interiors, in providing bathrooms, gas or electric cookers, balconies for babies, rooms for drying clothes, and new ways of disposal for refuse.'

As you have seen, millions of new homes were needed after the Second World War but bricks, tiles, timber, paint and other raw materials were in short supply. It took years before builders could build enough homes. This is why a decision was taken in 1945 to build the different sections of a house in a factory in advance and then fit them together on the site to make a prefab (prefabricated home). Prefab homes were cheap to build, warm and comfortable inside, and equipped with hot and cold water, bathroom, WC and kitchen.

A prefab in 1948. ⇩

⇧ Council estates built in the 1950s were often long rows of semi-detached houses.

⇦ In the 1960s, many councils built flats instead of houses when they began to clear the slums, like the tower blocks shown here in Sheffield in 1964.

Some homes were built by local councils. These council estates, as they were called, included many different types of home, such as modern terraced houses, tower blocks of flats, rows of semi-detached houses and bungalows, and small blocks of flats called maisonettes. In the 1980s, people who rented houses from their local council were given the chance to buy them, increasing the number of people in the country who owned their homes.

New building methods were also introduced after the Second World War, such as double-glazed windows to make homes warmer inside. Gardens were open plan with only low walls or fences separating one house from the next. The window frames of houses built in the 1930s had been made of metal. Now they were made of wood or plastic. Houses in the 1960s had very large 'picture' windows but many of those built in the 1970s had small panes called Georgian windows.

⇧ A house with large 'picture' windows dating from the 1960s.

After 1945, the government brought in laws to control the way in which houses were built. New homes could only be built if planning permission was granted. Green belt areas – where houses could not be built – surrounded towns and cities to stop ribbon development. The government also built a number of New Towns to accommodate many of the people seeking a home.

Changes in diet and health

Until the start of the National Health Service in 1948, most people dreaded going to see the doctor since they had to pay two shillings (10p) a visit – at a time when many workers earned less than £2 a week. Medicine, ointment and pills cost extra.

Home remedies when you were ill

'Working-class people seldom saw a doctor when I was a child. Mostly we used remedies that Mother had learned from her mother or something a neighbour suggested. When we had colds we had eucalyptus sprinkled on our handkerchiefs and on our pillows at night. Infections such as boils, sties and abscesses were very common. Many a time have I sat with a rag soaked in vinegar on my forehead to cure a headache. Aspirin and other painkillers came years later.'

⇧ An advert for a health remedy in the 1940s.

⇦ Rickets was a bone disease caused by a lack of sunshine and Vitamin D which can be found in more expensive foods, such as oily fish, butter and eggs. Rickets caused deformities such as bow-legs. This is a group of Glasgow children with rickets in 1910.

Gloomy slum homes, like those in the photographs on pages 4 and 5, were very unhealthy. Children deprived of sunlight sometimes developed rickets.

Many homes were infested with vermin, such as fleas, cockroaches, mites, lice, rats and mice. You could pick a bug up at school. This is why the school nurse inspected the children's hair at regular intervals for lice. Many children suffered from scabies, a skin complaint caused by a tiny mite which led to itching, reddish lumps and sores. Impetigo was another skin complaint affecting many children from poor homes – especially those where washing facilities were inadequate.

The water that people drank and used could sometimes be a cause of disease.

A country nurse talking about life in her village in the 1930s

'There was no main water. We all drank from the ponds or the pump or from some wells.'

In the 1930s most working people only had enough money, if that, to pay for their rent, heating and food. They had to be thrifty. This is why their diet tended to be starchy food, such as bread and potatoes, which helps to fill people up. They ate relatively little meat, fish, fresh fruit or vegetables since these were expensive. One woman recalled living on *'suet dumplings and soups'*. Another said *'You was the one to go hungry, not the children.'* Most people who lived in poverty at that time can remember the meals they ate then.

⇧ Women drawing water from a water pump in London's East End in 1930.

A woman living in a country village in Suffolk

'We were very poor in the early 1930s. My father was a horseman on a farm. We only had meat from the butcher's at weekends – the cheapest cuts. The rest of the week we lived on what my father caught whilst working in the fields: rabbits, hares, pigeons, pheasants, partridges.'

⇦ An unemployed family in London, 1939.

A man living in a mining town in north-east England

'The Sunday meal was the only meal we had together, and we always had the same thing: my mum used to make a Yorkshire pudding, the size of the table nearly, and suet pudding filled with leeks and wrapped up in pastry, and afterwards rice pudding, a huge bowl for six of us; it was all filling food. I can never remember seeing fresh fruit in our house.'

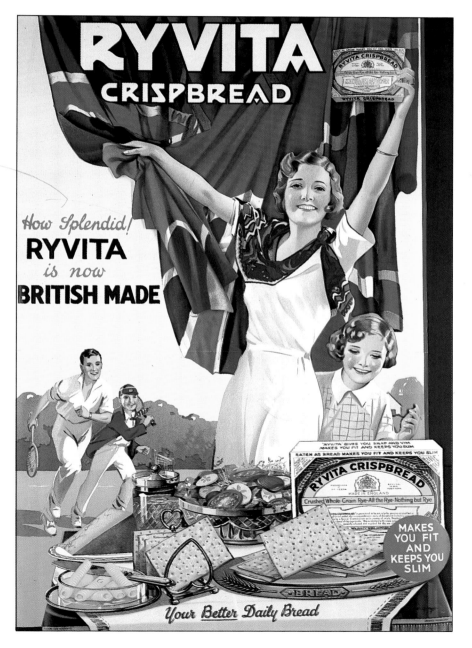

☞ Advertising campaigns for foods like Ryvita (1934), and Lin-Can vegetables (1952), were mainly directed at people from well-to-do homes who could afford to choose what they ate.

15

⇦ A child drinking milk at school in 1934.

In slum homes children often slept three or four in a bed made of flocks (cotton or woollen waste). Since the youngest often wet the bed, they stank of urine. The beds were usually the homes of fleas and cockroaches. In the morning children often went to school with red marks on their necks where the fleas had bitten them. People tried to keep their homes clean and used antiseptic fluids to kill the vermin. But they fought a losing battle in homes without proper heating, running water or an inside toilet.

Despite these problems, some improvements in diet and health took place before 1939. Because families were smaller, many people did have more money to spend on food for their children. From 1934 onwards, children could drink a daily glass of milk at school for only half a penny [0.2p]. Poor children got it free. The milk gave them some of the proteins, vitamins and calories they needed in their diet.

During the Second World War the government supplied free orange juice and vitamin tablets to pregnant women and cod-liver oil to their children.

Oddly enough, there was less, not more, food available once the Second World War was over. This is why rationing continued for nine years after 1945. People got used to queuing for everything. The government tried to get people to eat cheap food imported from abroad, such as whalemeat, Spam (a tinned meat made from pork) and tinned snoek (a tropical fish).

Vaccination and immunization, greater cleanliness and higher living standards as well as medical advances (such as antibiotics) led to a steep fall in the number of children catching serious illnesses, such as tuberculosis, scarlet fever, diphtheria, polio and measles. The National Health Service founded in 1948 gave everyone the right to free medical and dental care. As people became better off, so health standards improved.

Rationing food in the Second World War made people healthier since it ensured that the poorest families got enough food, such as 6 oz (170 g) of butter and margarine per person. ⇨

In the kitchen

The typical kitchen in the 1930s had an old cast-iron kitchen range. This was the name for a large coal-burning stove which heated hot water, warmed the kitchen and cooked food.

Many of the foods we eat now were available then. Prices seem very, very low compared with today but you should remember that average wages were lower than today, so people had less money to spend on food.

⇧ A kitchen stove in the 1930s.

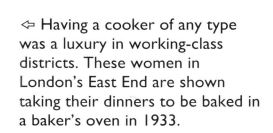

⇦ Having a cooker of any type was a luxury in working-class districts. These women in London's East End are shown taking their dinners to be baked in a baker's oven in 1933.

Food prices in 1933 (converted into modern weights and coins)					
1 kg bacon	8p	1 kg Cadbury's milk chocolate	15.5p	1 kg sugar	2p
tin of Heinz baked beans	4p	pot of Shippam's fish paste	4p	1 kg Lyle's golden syrup	4p
pint of beer	5p	1 kg self-raising flour	2.5p	1 kg tea	13p
1 kg digestive biscuits	15.5p	bottle of Rose's lime juice	10p	packet of Weetabix	4p
1 kg butter	11p	jar of Silver Shred marmalade	2.5p	bottle of whisky	60p
1 kg bread	2p	bottle of Lea and Perrin's sauce	5p	bottle of sherry	25p
1 kg cheese	15p	tablet of Wright's coal tar soap	2.5p		
Average wage of an ordinary worker in 1933 was under £2 a week					

The housewife in a working-class home had to be strong and tough. Water had to be carried in buckets from the cold water tap out in the yard. There was no running water inside the house – and consequently no bathroom and no flush toilet. Coal had to be scooped into a bucket and fed on to the kitchen fire – the sole source of heat in the house and often the only means of cooking available. Mats on the floor soon got dirty and had to be banged against a wall in the yard to clean them.

On washing days, a copper boiler was filled with water and heated so that steam filled the kitchen.

Washday in Norfolk in 1930

'I hated Monday. The copper fire was lit early, and then a ritual of soaking, washing, starching, rinsing and boiling commenced. The kitchen was soon full of bowls, tubs, baths and steam, and my mother was lost in misty clouds, or up to her elbows in soap suds, rubbing away.'

A Persil advert from 1934, but most people couldn't afford a washing machine. ⇩

The moment Persil soapsuds meet dirt or stains **they go for every speck with LIVING OXYGEN!**

THAT CLEANSING ACTION GOES ON UNTIL EVERY TRACE OF DIRT HAS GONE!

The minute Persil soapsuds touch dirt – it's like a miracle! Instantly they are seething round, soaking into it. In next to no time they've chased every speck of dirt away, leaving just clean pure fabric – fresh as the day you bought it. The reason is, Persil's soapsuds contain live oxygen.

As soon as they come in contact with dirt that cleansing oxygen streams forth – active oxygen with which no trace of dirt can live! That's the secret of Persil's extraordinary cleansing powers. That's why Persil gets everything so radiantly white – as no ordinary washing can possibly do.

Persil

The Amazing Oxygen Washer

In large families every day was washing day. There were always clothes to iron using a flat iron heated on the stove or on a gas ring. Housewives were envious of those who could buy a washing machine and an automatic wringer.

After the Second World War, more and more people were able to buy labour-saving devices to use in their homes as living standards rose and new homes were built. Many new types of domestic appliance became available. Twin-tub washing machines became popular in the 1950s and automatic washing machines in the 1960s. In 1964, it was estimated that one home in every three had a refrigerator. Every other home owned a washing machine. The development of detergents and new types of soap powder helped to make washday a less painful experience. As living standards continued to rise in the 1960s, 1970s and 1980s, people bought more advanced machines for their kitchens, such as tumble dryers, automatic dish-washers and microwave ovens.

⇧ A modern kitchen in 1938. Linoleum was a popular floor covering in the 1930s. It was easy to scrub clean using the long yellow bars of soap you could buy in the shops. Kitchens like the one in the advert usually had a number of separate units, such as a gas or electric cooker, water heater, fridge and washing machine. However, only a few people could afford kitchens like the one in this advert.

An advert for a Hoover vacuum cleaner and washing machine in 1951. ⇨

Progress in the Home

Hoover Limited take pride in the fact that their products are saving millions of housewives from hard, wearisome drudgery — not only in Britain but throughout the world. Wherever the name Hoover appears it is a guarantee of excellence.

THE WORLD-FAMOUS HOOVER CLEANER

The Hoover Cleaner, with its famous triple-action principle — " It beats . . . as it sweeps . . . as it cleans " — is undeniably the world's best cleaner — best in design, best in materials, best in quality of workmanship. There is a model suitable for every size and type of home.

THE MARVELLOUS HOOVER ELECTRIC WASHING MACHINE

The Hoover Electric Washing Machine has completely revolutionised the whole con-...ion of washing-day in the home. It does ...ull weekly wash for a large family and ...s such a handy size—suitable for even ...mallest kitchen.

VISIT THE HOOVER FACTORY
...sitors to the Festival of Britain are cordially ...vited to make a tour of the Hoover Factories at ...rivale, Middlesex, or Merthyr Tydfil, South ...ales, or Cambuslang, Scotland. Please write to, ...oover Limited, Perivale, or 'phone Perivale 3311 for more information.

...OOVER LIMITED

Factories at :
...ESEX · MERTHYR TYDFIL · HIGH WYCOMBE · CAMBUSLANG, SCOTLAND

Now she uses the new
Super-Soapy OXYDOL
because...

*...no other soap powder gets her
**WHITES
SO WHITE** –
without bleaching

This happy mother belongs to the Oxydol-white brigade. She's one of millions of Oxydol users who *know* super-soapy Oxydol gets their whites whiter than any other soap powder—without bleaching. They know, too, they can rely on Oxydol's rich, foaming lather to get their whole wash cleaner than ever before.

You can *see* the cleaning power in that lather. Those energy-packed suds come billowing up ready to do a thorough job right to the end of the dirtiest wash. Grimy overalls, grubby towels, sheets, shirts—the whole wash—all come up gloriously *clean*.

And remember—Oxydol contains no harmful bleach, no harsh chemicals. Join the Oxydol-white brigade today. You'll be amazed you can get such whiteness so safely.

NOW BETTER THAN EVER!

OXYDOL
A HEDLEY QUALITY PRODUCT

Oxydol

⇦ An advert for Oxydol soap powder in 1952, showing a stereotypical picture of a woman as a housewife.

Changes in clothes and fashions

The pictures on these pages show how clothes and hairstyles have changed since 1930. Bear in mind that these changes only affected people who could afford to buy new clothes. The clothes worn by very poor people were often second-hand, old or heavily-repaired.

⇧ Children with an unemployed miner in 1939, Wigan. Note the clogs on their feet and the dirty clothes.

This dress was designed during the Second World War when clothing was rationed. It cost many coupons to get a pair of trousers or a skirt. Utility clothing like this was very simple. ⇨

⇦ Women wearing mini-skirts at a race meeting at Ascot in 1968.

⇧ Typical hairstyle of the early 1930s – from an advert for Goodwin's toilet soap in 1933.

Recalling the fashions

'In the war years we wore our hair in a bun or roll at the back and wore shapeless trousers or dowdy knee-length dresses. Since clothes were on the ration you had very little choice. You made do with what you'd got. After the War came the New Look with its elegant long skirts. How we longed to buy one after all those years of rationing! The 1960s saw the biggest changes of all. We women had to get used to short mini-skirts. They were alright if your legs were nice!'

Hairstyles, too, have changed since 1930. Compare the styles of the 1930s with those of more recent decades.

A nightclub in London in the 1980s - punk hairstyles like these were first seen in the 1970s. ⇨

⇐ When servicemen left the armed forces, they were given demob suits like these soldiers are wearing, in 1945.

Men's fashions up to about 1955 were plain – a suit or else a sports jacket and flannel trousers. Macintoshes were long and often grey in colour with a belt. Most men wore their collars buttoned up with a tie. Very few men wore jeans.

By 1950, however, many more young men from ordinary homes were earning enough money to spend money on smart clothes. The Teddy Boys were among the first to do so. They wore smart suits based on Edwardian fashions – named after King Edward ('Teddy') VII.

Teddy boys in the 1950s.
⇨

In the 1960s, instead of having their hair cut cheaply – 'short back and sides' – by a barber, many men wore long hair and paid to have it styled by a hairdresser. London's Carnaby Street became world-famous for its clothes.

Carnaby Street, London, in 1965

'All down its narrow length the boutiques jostle each other. You hardly know whether you are shopping in His Clothes, Male, W.1 or Domino Male. It is the Mecca of the men, and girls too, who want one-step-ahead clothes and ideas, offering terrific choice of sharp, well-cut gear at fair prices. You can bump into people, as I did, such as Mick Jagger buying a sports jacket.'

Since 1970, choice of clothes has continued to grow wider. Jeans, leather jackets, sweaters, T-shirts, open-neck collars and trainers have become commonplace. In many cases, the differences between men's and women's fashions in clothes and hairstyles have almost disappeared.

Many men wore jackets without collars like those worn by their favourite pop groups, such as the Beatles, shown in this poster in the 1960s. ⇨

Changes in family life

Sixty years ago, it was quite common for people to spend all their lives in the streets where they were born. Few children from working-class families went away to college. People expected to get jobs close to their home. A writer on slum clearance said *'I know of dozens of families who have fought by every means in their power to avoid being moved even a mile or two from the district in which they were born and bred.'*

The Second World War had a big impact on families. Many children hardly saw their fathers during the war years. When town children were evacuated in September 1939, many families were devastated.

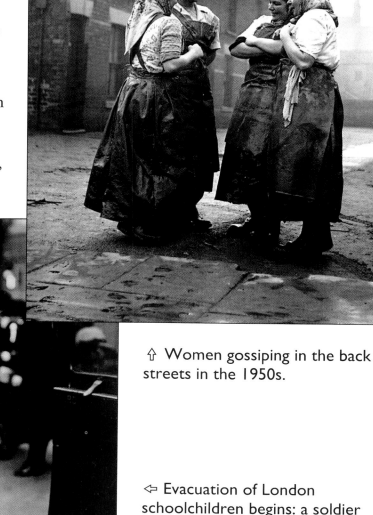

⇧ Women gossiping in the back streets in the 1950s.

⇦ Evacuation of London schoolchildren begins: a soldier says goodbye to his evacuee son in June 1940. Some children saw it as a great adventure but many sobbed themselves to sleep at night.

Families seemed to do more things together immediately after the war.

↑ Family tea in the 1950s.

> *'All four of us used to go to the cinema together – me, my brother, Mum and Dad. Other families did the same. You thought twice about cheeking your parents then, of course, not like nowadays. Mine never hit me but some of my friends were smacked or got the strap at home if they misbehaved. Each year we went together as a family to Bridlington – even when my brother and I were in our late teens. There was much less divorce then but that didn't mean that people had happier homes. Far from it. Many of my friends had to leave school at fifteen because their parents wanted them to start earning wages.'*

Most people were better off in the 1950s. There was little unemployment then. Most workers had a job. The extra money coming into people's homes meant they could afford to spend more on food and household goods and on their children. In 1970 the *Daily Mail* reported that: *'Every other family in Britain now runs a car and two-thirds have a washing machine and fridge.'*

Following in mother's footsteps!

⇦ An Oxo advert from the 1930s. Notice how the picture assumes, like most people did until the 1960s, that girls want to become housewives when they grow up!

As more and more women went out to work, families had to change. Some husbands did their fair share of housework and took on other duties around the home. To the astonishment of an older generation, some became house-husbands, doing the housework while their wife went out to work.

> *'I can't remember my grandfather or father ever doing any housework – apart from doing the dishes on Christmas Day. I don't think my father even knew what the inside of a grocer's shop looked like! He would be amazed to see my son changing nappies, setting the table, cooking exotic meals in the kitchen, washing up or hoovering the carpet!'*

Not all the changes were to the good. Replacing terraced streets by high-rise flats in the 1960s helped to destroy the feeling people had of belonging to a community. People were used to borrowing sugar, milk or tea and sometimes even clothes from each other. One person recalled borrowing a macintosh to go into town. *'You were never afraid to ask'*, she said. In a television programme in 1983, Salford women who had been moved from their terraced homes to a high-rise block of flats had angry words to say about these changes to their way of life.

'We didn't want to move.'

'You're stuck in a flat. You go up in the lift, you're frightened of getting mugged.'

'What's the use of all mod cons and everything else? No friendly neighbours. No future. Nothing.'

'You could leave the door open then and not a thing would be touched.'

Tower block of flats in Newcastle upon Tyne, built in the 1960s. ⇩

Glossary

Back-to-back houses Terraced houses which shared the same wall and stood back-to-back with a row of similar terraced houses in the next street.

Boutique French word meaning a small fashion shop.

Council house House built by a local council, usually on a large estate consisting of many houses, most of them semi-detached.

Domestic appliance A tool or machine used to do work in the house, such as a vacuum cleaner, refrigerator or food processor.

Evacuees These were the children (and some mothers) who were sent by the government into country towns and villages in 1939 because they were afraid Britain's towns would be bombed when the Second World War started.

Flat iron A heavy iron made of solid metal which had to be heated over a stove or over the fire.

Green belt Stretch of countryside surrounding a town. New houses and factories could not be built there, stopping ribbon development and preventing the sprawl of buildings into the countryside.

House-husband Man who does the housework while his partner goes out to work.

Immunization An injection (or drop of medicine taken with sugar) which helps to stop a person catching a disease, such as measles.

Impetigo A skin complaint often caused by unclean living conditions.

Kitchen range An old-fashioned coal-burning stove which heats an oven at the side and has a ledge in front for boiling a kettle. Usually black in colour.

Labour-saving device A tool or machine which reduces the amount of effort needed to do a job.

Lice Tiny insects without wings which suck blood and can live in human hair.

National Health Service System brought in by the government in 1948 giving everyone the right to see a doctor free of charge.

New Look Name given to the new fashions of 1947 which increased the length of women's skirts and dresses to bring the hemline much closer to the ankle than to the knee.

New Town A new town built from scratch in the countryside, or which greatly expanded an existing town or village.

Open-plan garden Garden with only low walls or fences separating one house from the next.

Pebble dash A rough surface used to coat the exterior walls of a building – made by spraying wet cement with tiny pebbles.

Prefab The shortened term for a prefabricated house – one fitted together on site from doors, windows, walls and other features ready-made in a factory.

Punk hairstyle The spiky and often brightly-coloured hairstyle worn by both men and women fans of punk rock music.

Rationing Method of limiting the amount of food, petrol or clothing any one person could buy in order to ensure that there were fair shares for all.

Ribbon development Name given to the way in which long lines of houses were built along the main roads leading out of towns in the 1930s.

Rickets An illness which weakens the bones and sometimes makes the sufferer bow-legged.

Scabies An itchy infection caused by a tiny mite burrowing under the skin.

Slum clearance Getting rid of poor, low-quality housing in a town.

Tower block Tall building with many floors (or storeys) containing a large number of flats or offices.

'Two-up and two-down' A small terraced house with two rooms downstairs and two rooms upstairs.

Books to read

Costume in Context: The 1920s and the 1930s by Jennifer Ruby (Batsford 1988)
Costume in Context: The 1940s and the 1950s by Jennifer Ruby (Batsford 1989)
Costume in Context: The 1960s and 1970s by Jennifer Ruby (Batsford 1989)
Costume in Context: The 1980s by Jennifer Ruby (Batsford 1991)
How They Lived: A Teenager in the Sixties by Miriam Moss (Wayland 1987)
How We Used To Live, 1954–1970 by Freda Kelsall (A & C Black, 1987)
Looking Back: Clothes and Fashions by Joanne Jessop (Wayland 1994)
Looking Back: Family Life by Jennifer Lines (Wayland 1991)
Looking Back: Food by Jennifer Lines (Wayland 1994)
We Were There: 1930s by Rosemary Rees (Heinemann 1993)
We Were There: 1940s by Rosemary Rees (Heinemann 1993)
We Were There: 1950s by Rosemary Rees (Heinemann 1993)
We Were There: 1960s by Rosemary Rees (Heinemann 1993)
We Were There: 1970s by Rosemary Rees (Heinemann 1993)
We Were There: 1980s by Rosemary Rees (Heinemann 1993)
When I Was Young: The Thirties by Neil Thomson (Franklin Watts 1991)
When I Was Young: The Fifties by Neil Thomson (Franklin Watts 1991)
When I Was Young: The Sixties by Neil Thomson (Franklin Watts 1990)
When I Was Young: The Seventies by Neil Thomson (Franklin Watts 1990)

Acknowledgements
Grateful acknowledgement is given for permission to reprint copyright material:
Page 6 *Town Children Through Country Eyes* published by the Women's Institute, 1940
Page 9 Article *London's ten-storey flats* by B. S. Townroe in *The Daily Telegraph*, 9 April 1935
Page 12 From an essay by Elsie Avery *In Those Days* edited by Julia Thorogood, copyright Age Concern Essex, Sarsen Publishing, 1994
Page 14 (above) From *Akenfield* by Ronald Blythe, the Penguin Press, 1969
Page 14 (below) From: *Suffolk: Within Living Memory,* compiled by the Suffolk Federation of Women's Institutes, 1994
Page 15 From the series *The Worst of Times* in *The Independent,* by Willie Hamilton, a former Labour MP, talking to Danny Danziger, 4 May 1992
Page 19 From *Within Living Memory,* compiled by the Norfolk Federation of Women's Institutes, the Boydell Press, Ipswich, 1973
Page 25 From *The Daily Telegraph* for 28 May 1965
Page 29 From BBC Television programme *British Social History: Twentieth Century Woman,* 1983
While every effort has been made to trace copyright holders, the publishers apologize for any inadvertent omissions.

Index